SCHOOL OF SUN POEM

EDWARD KAMAU BRATHWAITE

Sun Poem

Oxford New York Toronto Melbourne
OXFORD UNIVERSITY PRESS
1982

Oxford University Press, Walton Street, Oxford OX2 6DP

London Glasgow New York Toronto
Delhi Bombay Calcutta Madras Karachi
Kuala Lumpur Singapore Hong Kong Tokyo
Nairobi Dar es Salaam Cape Town
Melbourne Auckland

and associate companies in
Beirut Berlin Ibadan Mexico City

Brathwaite, Edward
Sun Poem.
I. Title
811   PR9265.9.B7
ISBN 0-19-211945-1

Set by Syarikat Seng Teik Sdn. Bhd.
Printed in Great Britain
by J. W. Arrowsmith Ltd., Bristol

James Edward 1844
Henry Lawson 1874
Edward Hilton 1908
Lawson Edward 1930
Michael Kwesi 1958

How could I, even if I chose
Now let another swimmer drown?
And how could I myself go down?

Francis King

CONTENTS

I

RED RISING

1

When the earth was made
when the wheels of the sky were being fashioned
when my songs were first heard in the voice of the coot of the owl
hillaby soufriere and kilimanjaro were standing towards me with
    water with fire

at the centre of the air

there
in the keel of the blue
the son of my song, father-giver, the sun/sum
walks the four corners of the magnet, caught in the wind, blind

in the eye of ihs own hurricane

and the trees on the mountain be-
come mine: living eye of my branches
of bone; flute
where is my hope hope where is my psalter

my children wear masks dancing towards me the mews of their
    origen earth

so that this place which is called mine
which will never know that cold scalpel of skull, hill of dearth

brain corals ignite and ignore it

and that this place which is called now
which will never again glow: coal balloon anthracite: into cross-

roads of hollows

black spot of my life: *jah*
blue spot of my life: *love*
yellow spot of my life: *iises*
red spot of my dream that still flowers flowers flowers

let us give thanks

when the earth was made
when the sky first spoke with the voice of the rain/bow
when the wind gave milk to its music
when the suns of my morning walked out of their shallow
    thrill/dren

So that for centuries now have i fought against these opposites
how i am sucked from water into air
how the air surrounds me blue all the way

from ocean to the other shore
from halleluja to the black hole of hell

from this white furnace where i burn
to those green sandy ant-hills where you grow your yam

you would think that i would hate eclipses
my power powdered over as it were

but it's hallucination my fine friend
a fan a feather; some

one else's breath of shadow
the moon's cool or some plan/et's

but can you ever guess how i
who have wracked

you wrong
long too to be black

be
come part of that hool that shrinks us all to stars

how i
with all these loco

motives in me
would like to straighten

strangle eye/self out

grow a beard wear dark glasses
driving the pack straight far

ward into indigo and vi
olet and on into ice like a miss

ile

rather than this surrendered curve
this habit forming bicycle of rains and seasons
weathers when i tear my hair

i will never i now know make it over the atlantic of that nebula

but that you may live my fond retreating future
i will accept i will accept the bonds that blind me
turning my face down/wards to my approaching past these
   morning chill/dren

II

ORANGE ORIGEN

3

i
With big black eyes in the face of his just-shaved too-big head
restless and thin
with his shirt-tail out of his wide white pants

the boy called adam came into the room

he had just come to town from the house in the country
brick brack plantation shack: his child was a slave there: where
when it was fine

he and his sister who was five played hide-an-seek
running stoopalong into the dark with its mystery glints and
    smells

and brushing cobwebs from their faces when it clung to their
    hands like sticky fingers

sometimes if the cobwebs came sudden
adam
who was taller than his sister who was five

would hit his head against the solid rafters above and a dull red
    love would glow in the dark

but what they liked best was to sit securely in the hiding dark
and marvel at the shower of green light around the gooseberry tree
and when mouse who was catcher

walked round the house and stood with her back to the
    gooseberry tree

her dress looked very white
and her skin against the gooseberry light

was smooth and bright
as if it had a life of its own
that lived in her skin that was black

they couldnt see her face
though they knew it was mouse
who stood with her back to the gooseberry tree

ii
adam had just come to town from the house in the country where
    these things were seen
and he felt so strange that he wanted to cry

there wasnt any soft green grass to run behind a ball
on
nor no trees he wanted to climb

if he hit his little tennis ball against the wall of his new home
if he hit his little tennis ball against the wall of his new home
too hard

it flew

quick as a sparrow through the window
and hopped hopped hopped on to the grey asphalt road of the street
    of his new home

and the cars were shining like beetles . . .

and the sudden green sun was a bright green ball that their wind-
shields crashed through the pains of his eyes . . . and their horns
were like sun on the windshields

again . . . but a sun that he heard in his ears . . . and the draught
of the sudden sights and sounds made his young head hurt

till he fell asleep under the glass of the street of his new home . . .

4

When adam awoke it was afternoon
and he saw a new light in the room of his new home

it was bright silver
and it danced up and down the wall that faced the open
  window

adam had never seen this kind of light before
but it seemed that the lines of light that faced the window
danced like the game of *buttons-an-string*

all the boys at school
had started to fix a button to a piece of string
and by twisting the string and pulling
it they could make the button spin and the string dance

the light on the wall was like the string in the game of *buttons-
an-string* only it was more spring an ting and there were many
more strings and many more speeds beyond what the best boys at
the game could do

nor there wasnt any noise: there wasnt any noise in this dance on
the wall. when he thought of the game of *buttons-an-string* he
thought of the throb of the game as well:

the small humming circle round the ones who played
riding and beating their horses to death
the boys at school always galloped their horses to death

sometimes when the teacher asked a question in class
it was a difficult task
to stop the boys not having to answer
the question they thought they could answer from galloping
  out of the class

but it wasnt like this with the water on the wall
for he thought of water though he didnt know why
when he watched the dance on the wall

and he wondered where the water was that made it walk the wall

    it was now spilling from the wall on
    to the ceiling in long swift leaps and jabs
    and with little pitter pointers pointing

    to the window opposite the wall
    where they had walked when he first awoke
    and adam watched the lines of light that looked like water
       lengthen into silver shadow

leaping and rippling leaping and lunging they fled leap by leap
through the window where the sky was big like a blue para
sol in the sun

              and he lay
              on his back
              and foll-
              owed the down-
              ward drop
              of the
              sky with his
              eyes
              that danced
              with the light
              of the room
              and his
              eyes
              climbed down
              the curve
              of the
              sky
              and fell
              like the
              sun
              on the
              see

allthekingshorsesandallthekingscoinswereprancingandscatteredin
lightontheseeandadamseyes flew upon andhisheartrushedout
tothesight he who had just come to town from the house in the
country hadthatbrightafternoon disco veredthe sea

III

SON

5

That he should come out of the dark
liquid like metal
leaven as a song

that there should be such silence
underneath his ripples
staining the blue

that there should be this pushing new
plumber of wings
stirrings in deep underwater rocks that can hardly see

that this lid should be so suddenly unlocked
this eye
open to a blood red road along the morning

that my son, so swiftly growing
his kite far out in heaven now

gravitation of hills, of fresh waves al-
most forgotten

umbilical chord of the dark muse his mother
barely unbroken

he rolls into high cloud, cool
breezes flow acoast the glitter bays of our devoted radar station

and yet at noon
he is the opposite of icicle, un-

bearably sheen; tumb-
eling through cloud into steel spots and anvil

glints

but he still knows that ice awaits him when the curve is done
down that descent he plotted on a rain-
bow: in the deep veins of neptune and uranus

on the hushed face of pluto
in the cold world of hydrogen candles
where the sea does not speak does not wash does not glow

i

Of all the beaches on the bay browns beach was the proudest
   place

big respectable houses of big respectable people looked on to the
   beach at browns bay

the pilot lived there

mr queen the big-able pilot who knew when the big ships came
and went far out in the bay with his tall

tail flag till his boat went down
where you watched from the shore to

only the tall tail flag that flew till the big ships came

mr queen was cock of the walk on the beach
for he brought great pride to the place

and his boat in the bay was the where-to-meet
for all the boys on the beaches about

they would splash with feathers of foam at their feet
and climb the gunwale of this meeting

place

they looked like ants on a piece of cake
and they sat and were happy like birds in a bush

ii

mr queen the pride of the place who didnt like ants
nor birds in his bush

would look from the window of his up
stairs room and call

to his man a de yard below
to chase de boys out-a de boat

his man had a limp and a wave
of hand as he rush

down the beach to do what his mas
ter said

hoi ...
> he shouted
>> across the smooth sunday water
>>> where the girls played shrill

hoiiiii ...
> he shouted across the blue wind-whipped water

>> to the boat
>> where all the boys from the beaches were still

hoiiii ... *dere* ...
> you black *&¼¼%! bastards* ...
>> *get out* ...
>>> *a de $**$ boat*

and his voice from the shore was a shake of their cake a stone in
  the bush

> and
> *chow*
went the water when the beach-boys jumped
and the water wore wreaths where they disappeared

> and
> *wham*
went the water when the land-boys jumped from the rocking boat
and they splashed up vines as they reappeared

i

When adam jumped he saw the akee tree and the tamarind tree

with the man-faced seeds and the coconut tree in the neighbours
yard and the shine on the galvanize roofs that looked on the bay

at browns beach and the men on the beach building pyramids and
the flash of the bat of the boys playing cricket and the girls playing
shrill in that part of the sea that ended with *wish* on the shore

and
the water went *chow*
as he closed his eyes

ii

when adam opened his eyes he saw the white sand coming to meet
  him through the huge sun

flowers that the light in the water made; so he bent his body out
of the dive and gilded along near the sand

it was quick, underwater, to swim near the sand;
and what with the clear petals of staring light

and the sprats about them like buzzless bees
he knew he wouldnt lose time nor his way

which was lighted and bright like a road on a moonlight night

dips and hills he passed that were smooth or covered with moss
and the sand was ribbed like water in wind and all was silent as a
  fish eye look

iii

he had come to the surface where the warm wind was
through the pale silver circle

that lay like a small life buoy
on the water where his head would bob

when a black hand fell like a bolt from the blue
and he sank like a ship in a thunder of foam

saw the sun-
lit soles of a bright boys feet as they pranced their war

as he looked through the bubbles
to the place where the live boy

lay

thats batto he whispered
as he moved his arms like water on wings

and came to the surface where the bright boy was

thats batto fuh true
as he came face to face with the shark that was lying in wait

i

Of all the boys on the beach batto was the biggest brave. best swimmer best diver best floater he was the shark of the sea-egg season and he ducked every boy he was sure he could beat any time any place without reason

he was the shake of their cake the stone in their bush. he was the boast of the beach-boys gang

batto came from the tumbledown village of low wooden houses overlooking the bay which stood on their stilts like a crab on its claws. where they nevvah had bottles rounn their garden beds

cause they nevvah had gardens an bottles were fuh fights an they was plenty plenty fights in de hickey. they could curse yuh muddah an ax fuh yuh faddah cause they didnt have mothers like the land-boys had an you couldnt curse they fathers who were fisher-men

batto never had a mother like the land-boys had and hed never even had to go to school. but hed been to dodds and hoped one day to go to a proper prison for the man who would cross his path so the beach-boys said

dodds was the place with the high barbed wire and the cat-o-nine tails far far away in the country. but your parents were vague if you asked where it was what it meant. you were told it was the place where the bad boys went

ii

when he was he didnt know how much then, batto had burss another boy eye in a fight

it was so:

you does stann toe to toe knee to knee and does stare at each
  udder
wid a fowlcock eye

then one is step back an tro dung e cap an comman
touch dat

but you isnt to look at de tro dung cap
but get back position in de fowlcock eye.

now batto bad bad bad when it come to a fight
an dis boy was a poor-great fool

so it happenin so:

de boy get a stone in e hann how uh doan know how
an batto when um start start out empty

but e step back quick an tro dung e cap an comman
touch dat

an de poor-great boy turn an look
when quick quick quick as a hen does peck

batto ups wid uh rock dat e feel all de time by e foot
an den murder start

e tek a step back wid de rock in e ann
an by de time de boy look back front

batto bark drop dat
to de stone in de udder boy hann

but de fool boy move
mek to puff out e chess when

bam

batto rockstone lann in e eye
so they senn e to dodds for being out-

lorded an de blood dat e bring pun de udda boy eye
so the beach-boys said

16

i

Adam now with his back to the land and the house where he lived
   saw the grin
flash bright from this rock that could fight this shark that could
   bite

his skin which on the beach was hard and rough and was spotted
   with salt
till it flaked like scales was smooth in the water and tight in the
   wind
and could carry a picture like a motorcar shine

and the sun was a medal on batto's chest
as he raised himself like water in wind
and his hands went high and quick quick quick as a hen does peck
they fell like a beak on adam's neck

it was bad bad bad as the sky went out and the water was flame
   over adam's eyes glass winked like a fallen star on the sand
and a shadow of garfish passed like a cloud
as batto held him down with his knees and his glittering weight

ii

with his back to the land and the house where he lived
adam wondered what
his mother would say if he didnt come back

and he thought of himself running up de black steps
the next day late for
school late for lunch late for

but if that was so he wouldnt be dead adam thought

iii

and adam thought of x/mas day watching his father open the
   wine. taking
the bottle between his knees his father had pulled till the cork
   went pop

now he was the battle between batto's knees and this pushing for
   breath was
the pull on the screw

but batto was shark in the bottle neck that kept bright hold on the
   screw

iv

*and adam can swim my sister will shout as i scatter the water
   about . . . about. . . .*

v

as batto ducked him again

vi

but this time adam touched adam caught adam held this boy who
was trying to beat him out of the water. looking back through the

blinding him bubbles he struck like a shark at the sea-egg shark's
belly pulled him down by the waist gripped his head and the grin

that was like a fire till they both dropped down together

beach boy and the boy who would be boy like the beach boys
were locked in the only way in the bay that could bring him his
spurs

and this was his wish as they hit the sand
and both were bottles at the floor of the bay

give in batto signalled
as the sky turned silver and the two lost time

give in batto signalled
as the ticking foam curled around them like vines

give in batto called
tugging at adam

lemme go lemme go lemme go

but adam held on and wouldnt let him go

18

IV

YELLOW MINNIM

10

i

The sea spoke to me softly of angels
but they were not white roses nor faery queens
they were black besses and bussas who came sculling over the
   reefs in their bateaus

the sun made patterns on the water that gave birth to children

the children, *mmofra*, sprats and sprays
tin charcoal sticks
eyes bright as sapodilla seeds are black

crack open with the suns glaze

and weep through the air like pollen of tears
their gold dust dies on the dry hillside
where an old woman, long patch work kente apron on the sky

line moves slowly with her hoe like a one leg

ii

the games we paid had little meaning
we were not hunters nor warriors nor even great lovers
we lacked the criminals

we picked up sticks seeds pebbles forgotten divinations

played romie or whist or suck-de-well-dry-dry
or draughts and dominoes
or monte carlo round the moonlight grass

lamp and felt the power of monopolys hotels

blue chips of wood: park lane mayfair the malls where rolls royce
    pawked
and grabbed our scouvenirs

and when the gas ran out we fell asleep along the deadwood race
    track underneath the kitchen chairs

iii
not knowing the names of our flowers and trees

scratchywhist womans tongue hogplum stinkin toe
we could only call our brothers robin hood or barnabas collins
we took white plastic bico cups

of ice cream bought
from the bico man in the light blue bico

van: cut

them to make serrated teeth of drac
ulas: we
fit the crescent up against our gums and waited

moush shut tight and ffull

when strangers passed and said hell

o: we let our eye
lids down and slowly un

dead: grinned

i
There are certain dreams that boys
have living by the sea
that they will become infamous sailors

see galleons whales
find treasure at the bottom of the ocean
tree; in the hills that they will climb

the mountain; in the desert ex-
orcize their god; in
my backyard that i will shift the boulder

brought years and years before
by the wet shoulder of torn
waves: grown older now and darker

no longer mossy
and in the jewel case of earth beneath
it: there would be this crab: tick-

ing scarlet: petties purple
frothing fromits from its shellac shell and shelter.
this was our vision of the ancient sun

squatting upon the sandy redge of memories
this crab knew ancient histories
old harbour cartagena tenoctitlan half

moon fort plantation grasses; re-
leased its scrapers scuttled with us back
to prisoned childhoods hintless of the world

of banks and bombs now voiceless auction blocks
but instincts fished for lay below the surface
with held and shining breaths that dived us down to truth

of ship retreating coastline dumbless origins

mosquito one mosquito two
mosquito jump in de ole man shoe

mosquito two mosquito tree
mosquito stick stick miss sally knee

mosquito tree mosquito four
mosquito knock in de donkey door

mosquito four mosquito five
mosquito six and de poor get lix

mosquito six mosquito seven
de man in de moon isnt livin in heaven

mosquito seven mosquito eight
mosquito nine rape de girl in de pine

mosquito nine mosquito ten
de monkey jump up and jump dung agen

aeyae yae jin jin *aeyae yae* jin-jin
monkey eat tobacco an shit

white lime

i

For this was the summer the blue egg'd blackeyed summertime.
red combs and proud bronze spurs now flared themselves in the
yards. blue white black brown fluffy and bare-necked hens scut-
tled and clucked in the seaside sun while slowly and tall/ly above
them turned and man/oeuvred the golden galleon cocks. for this
was the summer the blue egg'd blackeyed summertime. over the
fence of the seaward yards came the

sea-weed salt-sea sea-moss smell; and far away, where the fisher-
men were, the flying fish flew like corn that was tossed through
the drizzling air . . . sun streaks spread like webs over rock and
the patterned carpets of green purple grass where a crab scuttled
spotted with coral and pink and a starfish closed its eye. the whole
wild floor of the bay was like flowing so the dark rocks breathed
and the lighted seaweed

trembled. and there, cushioned and nested bright in the moss and
cracks of the deep green rocks, were the eggs you were diving to
find. and this was the difficult part: the picking. you had to be still
like a bee by a flower or a hummingbird over a fruit. then care-
fully cupping the palm a your hann so it wouldn't be pricked by
the prickles, you pressed on the sea-egg and pulled

it

lifting the white blue little hedgehog head from the rock like a cup
that is stuck to a saucer. *but hole it! doan mine if it tickle de palm
a you hann*: all the prickles are living: *but hold it*, don't mind if it
tickles the palm of your hand and down back down for another.
in the end you should have from two to tree pairs cradle into the
crook a you arm, each pair like de firs' one: face-touchin-face.

you is ress for a minit, holdin on to de rockin boat an yu breathin:
one two tree: and den down: is back dung under de water: all de
sky blue air you cud hole in you chess in you chess and de ress
store up in yu belly: eyes wide: eyes red: body curve down de
spine to hole de air better an give yu head time: *so is dung back
dung for annudda*: rock bruise prickle finger: rippin an robin an
rapin the ripenin blue egg blackeyed summertime sea

ii

and *tap tap tap* went the spoons off-shore: the men in the moses
    boats sitting off-shore breaking the sea-eggs shells

tap tap tap all the flat day long all in a row off shore

tap tap tap the men sitting cross-legged moored to the close-in
    shore

tap tap tap and the eggs were split opened lifted and turned
    upside-down so the

sea-moss salt-stale inside-shell fell onto the spattered floor
and the pure gold pale gold sea-egg roe were veins of the sea-egg
    shell

tap tap tap from the blue black boats blazed with the white living
    white waving light

of the heaped-up sea-egg shells and they cracked the egg through
    its one black
watery eye and their spoons raked the gold core clean. a full tin
    tot
was passed

to the shore with its conical gold-core head
and given a grape-leaf covering hat
by the sea-egg women who sat near the boats on the sloping
    browns beach shore.

and they rose from the sand when their trays were full and

sea-eggs . . . they sang
    eyes looking down as they balanced their trays . . .

            sea-eggggggggggg . . . looook me heyyyyyyyyy
                    swinging full sails of their hips from the shore . . .

24

i

In the great purple dawn the fishermen poured like priests to the shore. it was dark where they stopped, filling their cans with water that swished from the pipe like wind through a key hole: the tone getting deeper as the bucket filled up. then they moved on: walking in twos and in threes: tall black monks of the morning light wrapped in their cloaks because of the cold and their anti-salt-water coats; walking out of the night down the street ahead of the sun and under the leaves of the seagrape and cordia trees whose flowers were fast fading stars in the touching them softly light. and before the houses awoke, before fathers opened windows and doors, at the time when the first cocks crowed and the last dogs

barked at the passing ghost (so the housewives said) the fishermen were away . . . one handed sculling: oar at the back of their black moses boats: twisting and turning and making an eight in the water still suddenly bright with darkest-night bubbles and break-outs of light . . . a splash and a voice to a voice across water like a seine net tossed across silence . . . then the squeak and slide as the sail-ropes pulled through the pulleys and the brown triangles of sail went up, catching the wind and the tree-top light as the sky grew bright: mirrors to wind and to light . . . and so the fisher-mens wakes were wide and away before the houses awoke. each boat with its three priests huddled and humbled over a prayer: their steering eyes already miles down the rising horizon . . .

ii

but suppose the fish can live for ever
    adam thought

      as he opened his windows of eyes that were glass and sank to
        the tinkling sand

      the sand always tinkled when he dived near the shore
      as if the tide was a rope pulling bells little bells
      whose silvery tongues were two grains of sand

if i could learn to breed-in water like a fish
i could stay underwater for as long as i wish
better than all on the beaches about
i'd be sharper than sharks in the sea-egg season

i would duck whoever i like without reason
i'd be able to dive for the fishermans pots
and find my own way to the floor of the bay
without losing my way

adam thought

for he remembered going out in a boat one day
and trying to dive for the fishermans pots

but he couldnt get down

and the sea was as heavy as fishermans grub
and he lost his way in the dark blue tides

and he wondered if the story was true that man could ride
down the tides of the bay without losing his way

adam thought

*if i could made a bubble/if i could make a bubble in my mouth/i
would suck in air when i needin it/an breed back out in de
bubble/adam thought/cause thats what de fishes do/adam
thought/when they swims with open mouths*

iii

so soon after dawn when he came to the sea he dipped his head in
the close-in shore and practised making this bubble. he would
breathe out into the water and suck back fast hoping to take the
sea by surprise and suck back air instead. but the water struck
bright and flashed in his head when he tried to breathe-in air. and
sometimes he would whip up water the way his mother beat up
eggs: making the sea-salt foam. and taking tiny bubbles in his
cup of hands, he'd suck at them and blow at them: dripping

but *tick*
went the bubbles

tick tick
went the bubbles

and burst back to plain water . . .

and once before he went in to the sea, he took a piece of soap and
put it in his mouth . . .

all the children he knew rubbed soap on a cotton thread reel and
blew the suds into bubbles . . .

his mouth was the cotton tread reel . . .

but the soap stung like ants at the sides of his face: his tongue
big and smooth in the burning bush as he spat out like a fire . . .

i

Whatcha doin dat for
his little sister asked
as she stood by the window wringing out clothes

   whatcha doin dat for
for bubbles, he told her
   for what for, she asked him

for bubbles, he told her
   for why for, she pressed him
for z for, he said

   how funny, she told him
   moussin her nose
how funny, he followed

follow pattern kill cadogan
mek
a monkey brek e hann

   so five four three two
   out goes you
   she was laughing

i int goin anywhere an is bess
you start mindin you biz-
ness

   my biz-
   ness? my

   bizness! you int see i
   suddin dese cloze?

   she dipped her hands back down in the basin and rubbed
      them

you think, a-
dam started
you think

i cud dive from hey to de pilot?
    to de pilot?
    eyes opening out from her basin of blue
    to de pilot

    but it faaaaaar she said slowly
    travelling back homewards over the glistance
    you tink yu cud dive to de pilot?

dat's why adam said
i goin to have to invent
it

    in what int?

in vent it he told her
to breed underwater he told her
as if i's a summarine

    you's a what!

summarine.
cause den i cud dive
to de pilot he told her

    but a mahn cahn dive like a sum machine ting

rine adam said

    what?

rine adam said

    but a mahn cahn dive like a summa rine ting

who say so

29

i say so

but you jess got to know what yu doin

who say so

i say so he told her

but who say dat yu know what yu doin!

if i cud breed-in water like a fish
i cud stay underwater for as long as i wish
an-

nothin won't happen? this
submachine ting sounn fishy to me
an yu know yu isnt no fish

sister told him

ii
De lorry mek duss like a shirt-tail flappin an we swingin de corn-
ers fass fass fass an de trees dat we pass goin flick flick flick all
de way down to six mens bay

there was a long red flatform out in de sea and schooners wid sails
that was bigger than a tarpaulin sheets was droopin them down as
they edged slow slow to de pier for dat was de flatform name,
fillmore said

he had begged to go for a walk on this pier and oooh it did take
from as long as from hey to de hills it did take so long, fillmore
said

pun de edge by de enn a de pier, fillmore said, tree boys had a crab
an was hookin it pun a cotton-tread line . . . most like de cotton-
tread line you does nuse pun a kite, fillmore said, only this one
was nasty an black an wasn't enough to ball pun a stick, fillmore
said

dey tek dis crab an pull off e taws an stick haff e body pun a bright
hook pin they had benn an tie to de line, fillmore said, an nex ting
so they tek up dis line . . . one a de fellers tek up dis line . . . an
swing it an swing it . . . at firss short an slow short an slow short
an a little bit faster a little bit faster an faster an faster till it pick
up speed when e let it go . . . an it pitch like a fallin star . . .
fillmore said . . . an de line come clammy an straight in de palm a
de hann a de fellar dat trow, fillmore said

then he sit pun de edge a de pier wid de tread in e hann while de
udder two trow deirs too, fillmore said

an they all sit still like a stone pun a hill while he watch them so,
fillmore said

den all pun a suddun: so suddun like buddum: de feller who firss
trow de line jerk quick wid e ann at e wrist . . . like dat . . . jess
like yu jerks yu wrist when yu kite does pitch an yu voo voo voo
an begin to haul in de belly an slack a de line till she straighten
out, fillmore said . . .

it did juss like a kite dat does pitch an toss when it tail too short,
fillmore said

but de boy haul it in wid never a word . . . jes like yu hauls in a
kite when it tail too short, fillmore said

an de udder two went on sittin . . .

an de fish was bright when it lann pun de pier: a shiney blue
colour wid plenty black dots goin flip flip flip wid it tail all de
time pun de wood a de redwood pier, fillmore said

and the air was a fish where his arms were wide

an de boy benn dung an prise up e mout an pull out de pain dat
did hide up inside all de time in de snout-fish tongue if a fish have
tongue, fillmore said

31

an de fish jess stare like francis who bline...an flip flip flip went e tail all de time pun de pier, fillmore said

and de tings at de side a rit face dat did look like ears...though they wasnt ears ... fillmore said

jess open an shut open an shut an yu cud see like fire inside ... then it stop, fillmore said

this summarine ting musse work like a fish adam said

15

But *how can fishes live for ever!*

if they are not hooked he told her
cause they breathe-in water an not die

    you lie!

you tell i how i lie he told her

    cause everything that live muss die!

not everything he told her
sea don't die

*cause batto faddah say dat when e out in e boat all day e does
   feel de wind dry*

*an de light goin out an de stars beatin an big like they want
   to drop outa de sky*

*fore de sky turn to red an de winn rise up an wheel ever
   ting back rounn to mornin . . .*

*but de sea e say not since e born days e say nor de days before e
when e faddah sail a fishin boat an batto faddah faddah live to be*

a hundred batto say

*not since before dat time nor rafter batto faddah say e faddah say
e nevvah know de sea to stop nor strange* adam said

*and i sure de fish dat live deep dung far out out there can go on livin
like dat too* adam said

    flyin fish too?

wha happen to you!

    int they live far out/an they dive deep dung?

and he remembered going out in a boat one day and trying to dive
  for the fishermans
pots . . . but he couldnt get down and the sea was as heavy as
  fishermans grub . . .

> *an yu   know*
> *an yu   very well know*
>
> *they is fine them lyin   an dead*
> *pun de sea on a busy flyin fish day*

tha is true a-
dam said still finding his way through his sister's wit

> *as yu   know/as yu   very well know*

but is birds he
began she

> was laugh
> ing: held up her hands with the white soft soap feathers

they is birds he
start/ed again

> *no man* she was laugh
> ing *fishes an wishes an birds!*
>
> *it int natral man* she was laugh
> ing

yet she loved to think them trying to be birds trying to leave the
dark heavy water dragging the links of the chains of the water,
poor slaves, a little bit higher and higher and higher till their fins
skimmed the surface and the chains dropped back dripped back
and their flish felt the air saw the prisoner sea for the first time
there wider and wider below them saw with wonder the tide flow-
ing forward and farward smelt the salt knew the irksome ache of
the scales on their small drying flingers now wings as they tried to
flip tried to flap tried to rise . . .

34

it wasnt natral but they wished it and she wished them wings as he would seek their secret bubble as he called it no matter what his sister said

but he didn't reply swallowed hard: hearing more in his head than his heart could hold

     an all dis depenn pun a bubble!

he drifted down humble

     poor yu   an yu   bubble
     poor yu   an yu   trouble

was he down was he drown was he drown/ing

i doan know why i is bodder wid you
you is only a girl an cahn unnerstann what i sayin

     wuh!

     she shout out
     her hands stopping scrubbing

     wuh-dah!
     her eyes dark and shining

     i is only a oooooooh!
     she cried as if suddenly dreaming

     look!
     she cried

     out

     look man!
     she cried

     out

look look look look! her eyes wide
look look look at it man! her lips pout

ed

a bubble had blown from the reel while he boasted
it burned very blue very blue while it lasted

turning around like the world on its axis
holding the light like a little lamp burn

ing stood there still for a bright moment turn
ing then *like it burss*! she said learn

ing

Bubbles of the world
sky blue moonlight

the sons of the earth ignore dreamers

    faced with bone iron steel in their pillagers
    they work long lines of rock cutters

    harrowing steps up the steps of the cit-
    adel terracing fields to the factory
    lifting tuned stone

bubbles of the world
sky blue moonlight

there is a girl at the window
her flesh of cheek reflects the sheen of shadow
green tangerine young black

but the sons of the earth ignore dreamers

    knowing their women soft only at the moment of generation
    but always hard with word with nag with shrew
    with thistle plimpler thorn and hoe

    and

crack: it will be dolour
hump: it will be bread
hah: it will be banging bell and bottle

sweat: it will be gristle
blood: it will be hoom of ashes
tears: it will be guitar strings upon my father's skeletone

the sons of the earth working in long rows
                     in long chains
                     in long queues

barbecues of grit grief lip   printless word

shieldless with scars   without scimitars

scheming   but without plans

working towards their shadows palaces of cold

and

crack: it will be no pillow
hump: there will be no gold upon that head
tap: it will be the dregs of future glory

V

THE CROSSING

17

i

When adam walked out on the long redwood pier of his thoughts he found a new world opening out inside as a fishermans boy finds a new world below when he pulls his line from the sea wet with sea-weed and sea-moss and shadow and a lashing fish on the tail

adam at nine was growing both ways: up so his mother had to give him new shirts and her friends said how tall he was getting: down to the darker soil of himself fitting himself to new feelings. he was noisy on top where he faced the sun and the sea-wind breeze where the warm world was but inside growing down like the roots of a tree he was silent having no words to nourish that darker feeling

and adam found that growing up at nine towards the battoes on the beach towards the boys at school towards the heat of meeting for the first time people that he had not known before was more exciting somehow than this growing down was more like wind in shak-shak trees called womans tongue than like the tall grey sighing ghosts of mile-tree casurines whose travelling up so high so soft was like the push and quiet in him growing down

for growing up was finding for the first time there was other sea behind the high hills of the island's other shore: at bathsheba and cattlewash: the ragged coasts where the sun came from

ii

to cattlewash on the sunday school excursion . . .

expectation blowing up like a balloon for weeks before until at last: d-day: bank-holiday: with all the boys in coloured home-made shirts now blowing out behind like yellow pink red blue balloons. . .

o all the best buses in the world were there

sunny loo . . . black belle . . . breakneck jane . . .

iii
aaaamen
to the godspeed prayers in the church and then they were off

looking at everything they passed/shouting at everything they passed/clapping at everything they passed/bugle horns blowing as the world unfurled . . .

the jumping houses/the hedges in bunches/telephone poles like slim/crucifixions dip up/dipping down/shining black wires/dip up/ dipping down/thread on a spool . . .

we're going to a wonderful place
we're going to a won der ful place
over the hills and far away
we're going to a wonder full place

the jumping houses/the hedges in bunches/scampering lady-hens/ lifting their skirts/ fields spinning past them/like painted wheels/ green red brown/green yellow and brown/the lanes between them/ turning like spokes

we're going to a won der ful place
we're going to a wonder full place
over the hills and far away
we're going to a wonderful place

o the trees and/the breeze and/the fields spinning past clear/holiday weather/and mother behind in the following bus/with baskets of sweet-drink and/conkey and/ham so they shouted when/there was shouting to do/ and sang nearly all the songs that they knew/and they clapped and were happy like birds in a bush/till well away in the morning

All the boys in the sunday school bus lived on the sunset side of
   the island

where the land was low and the sea was calm except in september
   when the hurricane
season roof-ripping cane and the fishermen hauled their boats up
   the beach as high

as their boats would go. but the rest of the year it was calm. the
   west
of the island was calm. the land where the little boys lived
was as calm and as green and as soft as the sea at low tide

if you went far out in a boat on the sun
set side of the eye/land: looked
back: shifting yourself in your seat to look

back

you would see how slowly the houses were drowned
how the light of the beaches went out
how the land that you loved like your mother

seemed to sink under dark choppy water
that was ringing you round like a wall

looking back to the land
you would see that only the tallest trees were still
standing

but they were losing their colour
but they were closing their names
they didn't toss light anymore

and the hills behind them were smokey and smoothe
as if no grass or outcroppings of rock
silvered and littered their hopes anymore

slowly they dipped up dipped
down steadied and slowly
dipped down again: be

coming part of the water: be
coming part of the dream

until they were almost not there
like old men . . . being forgotten . . . dozing away into silence . . .

but when the boat nodded back
they were suddenly green and sharp and alive again

into the dream   of the water
into the dream   of the world

till the sun and the sky and the whirl where they were
was one with the spot where they were

but always they knew (all the little boys knew)
that the hills on the other side of the eye

land

stood ragged and fear and red in the sky/like thun
der made visible

and the sea over there was a giant of i:ron
a rasta of water with rumbelling muscles and turrible turrible hair

i

Hearse hill was the hill that the bus climbed now

one wicked man could make the bus stall make the brakes give
way so the wheels would slip back slip back down faster and fast-
er faster and faster and faster and faster until they crashed
through the wall at the side of the road and topple over and over
and over and over waaaaay dung dung to de gully . . .

ii

so shak shak excitement gave way to a different excitement as the
buses entered the hills

iii

      up . . . up . . . up . . .
      the engines droned up . . .

      trees leaning closer
      and closer and closer across the sides of the road . . .

      watching the hemmed-in boys in the buses . . .
      whispering . . . watching . . . watching and waiting . . .

hearse hill

      everyone quiet/no clapp/ing no/gladsong
      only the sad sad song of the doomed and clambering bus

hearse hill

      the little boys sitting now bolt upright
      heads straining forward

      who was the wicked one/where was the wicked one
      better keep the eyes shut/eyes shut tight

hearse hill

is it me o lord? is i is the one?
dear god if it isnt too late to pray lemme pray

i dint mean to do/it
i didn't mean to do/it

and still the bus shuddered

hearse hill

PLEASE DOAN LEH ME DIE STOP DE BUS LEH WE
  TURN BACK NOW I WAN TO GO HOME WAN TO
  PEEEEEE

butthebusdronedupwardandon

hearse hill

trees . . . leaning closer . . .

trees . . .

brushing against the sides of the buses/making a noise like the
  sea on the lonely coast of the night

hearse hill

droning and drowning-them-wickedly-trees surrounding them
  blinding them/shutting them in

hearse hill

and/*slip*
    went the wheels
          you-will-slip-back-down-to-the gully

and/*slip*
    went the wheels
          you-will-slip-down-into-the-dark

44

curse hill

    youwillslipdownintothedark

worse hill

    sunny loo black belle breakneck jane

    when sudd/enly

light

    coming in

crash

    like a stone breaking glass and

oooooooh

they gasped all the little boys gasped as they saw the blue tilted air
and the sea standing up like a green blue purple and shimmering

wall and far far below so far far below that they gripped their
seats was the promised land

VI

NOOM

20

When the sun shone on the polyps
they became shells
and before the fish had rippled scales over their spongy flesh
the skulls had become hills

and the hills grew green as the grass took root and flourished

a ship came, seeking harbour, fleeing from torture and swords
and a sugarcane sprouted
it grew taller than the crab grass and the nettle
it grew taller
and its owners shouted for their women to behold this sibilant
   miracle

they brought knives and cutlasses and bill hooks and baskets
hoping to reap rich harvest
but the sun was too hot and their waxen flesh
melted like candles of fetish or faith within their wooden churches

they saw their profits recede like hope or mirage
and they worried about their courage
and that the brown island might become a green desert of fields

some deserted the coral
and fled to more flattering glacial land/scapes
fishing in nova scotia sharpshooting injuns along the navajo trail
refrigerating their meals

the ones who remained grew black in the face
and their grey folded thoughts turned to africa

there were tribes there of scarecrows
hunters of heads who ate humane bones
crink skull and cavicle

big buttock women who preferred to mate with baboons
orangoutangs who ate oranges like well trained children in our
    zoos

they knew maize: yes: and yam and cassava
could fashion aztecs of beads to cover their naked zon-
goes were skilful with muddum and clayfish

they used wood well and pounded their grain into their own
fashioned mortars: were mortal
and worshipped the devil like

henry viii, like leo x, like francis i, like pope joan
of arc, like baptists, like jesuit priests, like ni-
collo machiavelli like the niggers they were

they caught alligators to make tooth
charms against the spine-
ache: against spear thrust and man-

drake
but they didn't know bulls barcelona or bullets
they couldn't claim comfort of clergy

fine

we'll let columbus deal with this matter: he has three ships
that will import them: the *nina*
will take six hundred from senegal
the *pinta* will take on five thousand — the boatswain will make
    them

hold

at the côte d'ivoire and the gambia;
and the admiral's caravel flagship will sail on down the coast
crossing the terrors of equatorial miasma
until it reaches the tong of the congo

it will throttle its anchor down into the cold muddy morn
    ing water of the man-
grove swamps and manacles and it will wait:
sooner or later a man with a fan, or a lion or loin cloth, bare
foot or in pal:anquin will rise to the bait

mumbled by drummers and several fearful attendants
do not run
abate them with bullet or bribe:
better bribe if you can

preserve the bullets for naygars
and bring back a hundred thousand:
this isn't no joke
remember what happened to raleigh and drake

above all, love
ignore their songs their manimal membranes resounding with the
    sounds of their godderel
and don't try to learn their langridge: teach them spanglish
preach them rum

ignore too the customs of their courts: the loaves
of their bread do not float on the water: what you break
you must eat: therefore

do not seduce the headman's wife but his cook:
what he loves he will flart: look
to it: your cock might depend upon

it

and there are certain noblemen, their priests, you might call
them, who talk too much and mutter and make zodiac
signs and have, you will find, a great deal of influence
among the warriors and older women

stick knives through their tongues
and when the ship sails for the fair winds of the azores
strangle them drunk and dunk them overboard
the dolphins will weep while the sharks rip their watery groves

i

From the very left of the curving land the rocks rolled down to the

sea down from the dark troubled hills over which the sunday
school buses had come down past the few bent coconut trees

down past sad clusters of sea grape and cactus the match stick box
houses and over grey grasses woven tight and tough as a mat on
the shore the tumbelling rocks made their way

ii

it had happened a long time ago said the cattlewash boys longer
ago than uh nevvah remember when the *loa* came out of the sea
the sun shining down and everything peaceful when they lifted
themselves loudly heavy and darkly out of the water chasing their
dreadren out of the sea... as he fled said the cattlewash boys
he grew taller and taller pushing the water before him bringing bad
weather ashore ... coming in slowly loudly and legba ... it took
half a day before he could reach the shore ... and imagine said
the cattlewash boys how he must have felt when he reached the
shore ... the sea-wind cold on his belly giving him plimpler ...
the sea-sand sucking and soft at the soles of his feet ... the grind
of the pebbles and shells under his stumbling weight ... how his
toes must have twitched for the first time then on the new hard
shiny beach ... how he must have paused in that sky-blue air
before making the effort ... bending forward a little ... hands
gripping and pushing against his knees ... climbing the slope of
the sand ... how he must have made huge prints in the sand ...
his wet weight pushing it into deep valleys and dunes as he
laboured over the sand ... once he had stopped turned looked
back at his home ... at the sea and the distant thinder of guinea
... feeling the noise of the water he had come from drying from
his shoulders from his neck and belly ... feeling slow trickles run
down his hair and his thighs like mollusc or manawar jelly ... to
drill little drips in the sand ... and standing there by his now lost
home he must have felt his smoothness going from him ... he
must have felt his body lose its shining... as the water that had
always loved him now died on him ... the sea salt going white as

ashes on his lids and lashes . . . and standing there still and look-
ing there longing he would have seen his brothers watching . . . *ga
dagomba dogon dahomey* . . . dark and dangerous outlines on the
silver line of the horizon . . . heads and shoulders . . . islands low
and humped on the new now lowering horizon . . . for a long long
time he had watched them so . . . not hearing the waters . . . not feel-
ing the sea sharpened wind that was peeling his eyes like its salt
peels a paling as he watched them there . . . knew for the first time
fear: he here: they watching him faraway:

there

so he had roamed said the cattlewash boys raging along the thun-
dery coast tearing the trees uprooting foundations of quietest rock
tumbling boulder on boulder until they resembled his anger

but he never moved far from the shore nor the sound of the sea

and when his raving was done he had stood on a cliff called hack-
letons cliff and gazing full at the sun that was beating tormenting
drums in his head he had raised his head in a shout so loud it had
entered the gullies and rocks and was heard in the hills and howls
of that place with a sound of wind in a cavern

it was noon

and his cry grew greater as the pain of the world grew black for
him and he staggered and fell slipped staggered and fell down
hackletons cliff down past the few bent coconut trees down past

the clusters of sea-grape and cactus and over the grasses woven
tough and tight as a mat on the shore where he finally crashed

falling full length in the water

he dead where yu stannin now said the cattlewash boys

i

Soon after the blacks arrived plantations prospered
rivers of green flowered through valleys and up into the hills

white stone houses with green roof tops appeared
windmills retaining walls aqueducts

the slaves built themselves boxes of limestone
with black wooden shutters

pumpkin became divine
eke eat edge yourself slowly towards the borders of freedom and
    love-vine

in the grey cage of razor blade heat they sometimes glimpsed the
    sea
but the sky was too hot to be heaven

only at evening: the thin shave ice of the moon
the leaves of wind tinkling like glass in the cool of the seven stars

> sun have you forgotten your brother
> sun have you forgotten my mother
> sun who gave birth to shango my uncle
>   who was fixed in his place by ogoun the master of iron

> sun who blows the elephant trumpets
> sun whose hot nostril bellows in the bull
>   testicle birth-sperm love-shout origin

> sun who has clothed arethas voice in dark gospel
>   who works on the railroad tracks
>   who gave jesse owens his engine
>   who blue coltranes crippled train

>> remember us now in this sweat juiced jail
>> in this hail of cutlass splinters of cane
>> in this pale sail of soil

ii
but fear of the rat
    of the black
    wrack of africa

    ruins of dreamers
    conrad and kurtz

    rat-a-tap rat-a-tap rat-a-tap tappin

fear of the past
   not

    knowing it per-
    fumed or nas-

    ty: hear-
    ing about it

    only in whispers
    bound to the mast

    of streetcorners
    barbershop rumshop

    gossip in
    pissicle places

    after the sea-surge
    of young women's thighs

    combing hair
    between old women's sighs

    in the spittle of grandfather's pipe
    in his sneezes of snuff

fear of the graveyard ships
   clink coffle coffin

fear of the benin bronze
    of ifa's divination
    of maasai's mask of milk and bleeds

    running all life from the waves
    from the silver shadow of strife-
    heavy water

    turning the houses away from the landscrape
    ignoring the language of beach bus and gutter
    scavenging utters that were always our own

    like a rat like a rat like a rat-a-tap tappin

the sun is a curved glass that smokes
that bores holes in leaf and paper
that destroys archives and the parchments of industry

it is a baas eyed gaoler keeping our people back

    like a rat like a rat like a rat-a-tap tappin
    like a rat like a rat like a rat-a-tap tappin

    an we burnin babylone . . .

23

So one day leapin ahead a de governor dogs
turning malitia on to itself
wrappin dem up in de hickey like hell
cuttin de tongue a de backra man bell

was dis short stoutish fella who come
penny hole in sin philip
wid a big bushy head duh call bussa
gorbli he cud crack yuh cuss words like a cur

nul yuh hear: no
stoppin him hey since washington come:

                    good lookin mulatto good nigger gone
                    bad but not baaad like bussa was bad

i remember de nite two days after we brek up outta dis meat
box an de war declare from ev: ry hill/ top a de thundery heaven
dat ringin we rounn from long bay right away dounn to shark
rock an we cramp up an waitin under de man

                    grove near heddins: not
                    a soul in de sky but a few star
                    fish an de scar of a bleedin

                    moon: not
                    a clink in de fire
                    fly light: not

                    even no stamp nor a stammer
                    a horse: no
                    body not even ridin a hearse in dis

                    brave tomorrow we grave
                    yard: an de rain start to fall
                    so dat not even a canefields int burn

in not even at lower es
tate: dough we hear wid de sett
in sun dat ma

litious man com
in wid rounders: dem
big-able guns: dem ten

pounders: an i know
dem ignite
any one a dem booms

in my arse: is de lass
any one a dese rabble
raise slaves

who say dey is rebels an breth
ers ever hear
in from i an i mannin a

gain

so i ketch a quick pee an eeee
se out a fart
when dis fatty dark body
bounce me in true

an before a cud lann back good
pun me roots he start
in to talk an ole
man it wasnt no sky

lark

                    you
                    evvah see so much shite

he was shout
in   but soff
ly   he mout
hard

ly open

　　　　　you
　　　　　evvah see so much shite from where

　　　　　you come from to live hey? all
　　　　　　　dem white
　　　　　people pullin foot all de way up
　　　　　　　from hagg

　　　　　ets an turners hall woods jess
　　　　　to come up an lie dung hey in de dew

　　　　　an get bite up by spinks an moss
　　　　　keetoes as if dem is jew-boy

　　　　　or naygars who loss? why de rass
　　　　　dem cyan stann in de place

　　　　　dey belongs to an dead in dem bed
　　　　　wid dem boots

　　　　　on!

　　　　　why dem cyan stann home an
　　　　　　play wid dem poodle or
　　　　　pus t'rowin lu

　　　　　do or fire
　　　　　in darts but lissen to i bong

　　　　　o man

dis man say ketch
in a slap pun me shoulder dat pitch
me dark dung de hill like a boulder all
most

we gine block evry blow dem can pelt
  like a stick
man we gwine bite dem like
    shaego or shark

cause all a man want in dis worl
is de peace a e pipe an a lit
tle tobacco or ganja or snuff
an e umman

an de right to walk or ride bout
    dis parish
wid a fair field under de eye
a e foot an no favour

here i was wid dis piss
water hot
by me toe: if
not fraid den a ready to freak

out: an to tell yuh de trute
muh belly feel weak:
uh wus only willin to fight
cause a frighten:

when dis man who to
morrow dem lick
off de horse e was ridin
an ketch an chop

off e head wid a *plax*
at one blow
when dem ready
jess grumbellin dat

              e gettin no sleep
              cause de moss

              kitoes bite
              in wid nev

er a scare dat de gov
ernor come

an de white
people vex

dat we fight
in instead a flight

in from dem jess be
cause a dis man

who couldnt care less
bout defeat: wha name so:

e mane bussa

24

But heroes were in books
and few of our fathers were heroes

and we their sons learnt mainly to survive
although a few went out and fought
or spoke brave words from pulpits

and when they died
(the few who fought or spoke brave words from pulpits)
only their mothers treasured them
their helpless fathers looked away ashamed they could not do it

leaves leaves leaves   of a forest gone silent
leaves leaves leaves   without tongue without eyes
leaves leaves leaves   sun glut and gold and roten

when one of us made the monuments
then it was brass balloons and military music
parades and peacock feathers

women in their sunday blessed
clap cold and catalogue
grave stone museum dust

but those that drone their lorries all day up the sweating hill to the
    factory of mister massa midas
those mindless arch

itects that cut the cane
that built their own hurts on the hillslide
block upon block brick upon black of wood

and those more fortunate artificers who commanded the fury of fire
forging the muscleman force of the axe ringing the anvil
bending down to the crippled force of the ox
rising up singing

these and those who built canoes sculls schooners
those who could peel and plane sandpaper cedar

carving out rockers and glimmering banqueting tables and chairs
men who could mend roofs climb trees haul up the fishnets
     of their all-night silver home

there is still no brass movement or monument
to those headmaster backyard schools
who got up dawn each morn
ing to fuel

a promising scholarship pupil with words
with latin verbs with white hope with the right
rote

there is still no memorial epigraph
to those thick-set quick-step groundsmen
who watered the crust of west indian cricket

the sports day masseurs with canadian healing oil
the cork hatted sanitary in
spector with gauge and his dip-stick re

          membering when ever he wished: that
          regulation a chapter 3 section c
          contradicted b chapter e section d

          and that neither applied be
          cause your mother had no sewers no
          running water in the swollen hut

          no chain to flush the chinks away
          no valium against the jumbie fly and fall

ing wickets

and yet there are those stammaments in stone
that smile

are fat or romanesque, athletic like good traffic
cops

piercing or blind to the world but never look
ing like us

VII

BLUE LOA

25

Hannibal heavily crossing the alps
        clangour of armour, clamour of ice
        ravings of rock, steeples of metal green

        plunder

Hannibal heavily crossing the alps
        enamoured with honour
        risking his vigour on the slippery slopes of an elephant's

        thunder

        what sibyl slipped him that glacier
        how from his yard did he dream of that mountainous
           conquest
        how tall were the trees that he saw from the poor of
           his house

        was his father born lame: bit by machines: crushed by
           a god
        would the handclaps of vodoun have roused him
        did his drums dream those empires ump

Hannibal heavily crossing the alps
        was his father my farther setting out in his mental
           canoe

VIII

CLIPS

26

i
The sunrise was his cock and throttle
throat of a new day his old woman
conceptions taking place sometimes between midnight and creaky
   dawn

midmorning with his sons on sunday
out walking going for drives
just sitting around reading playing games

teaching them how to make windmills from cane
fly
kites sail
paper

boats milk
goats wash
dogs drive
stakes around the wounded fragiles of the flower garden

at noon his hat hot looking backward up to heaven his
   achievement
he sweats and smiles oil

merchant bank bal
ance health insurance premiums se

cure: his mis
tress or his mistresses will prove

it: the wife
has dwindled in that zenith hour

though it is she who drives the children on
while he awaits his honours

if they do well they are his just
reward

if they begin to fail
there will be time to rescue them with dis

approval

ii
the afternoon of fathers going grey
soft in the head
    in the belly
    in the heart

and where it hurts him most
    is filled with looking out of windows
    waiting for the bells to ring
    bring news of recognition

    the medals he had worked for worked for worked for
    that he praise god was not forgotten was forgiven
    the major breakthrough not the major breakdown
    and the report that turns out better than was feared

the afternoons of visiting the doctor and the bank
the pharmacist and friend and the conniving quack
and filling up the time with lodge and talking with the lodgers
and o shit not again cyan get de dyam cyar start

and wondering if the next days play is worth it
and trying to avoid the mistresses
and getting grateful to the wife
and hoping that the sons will rise up better than their fathers...

iii

that of course was the secular bourgeois family man of the
    property owning class
not much but enough
the butt and monument of the post-modern modernists and the
    pre-lenten leninists

there is you need not say i say the christian father of the family
temperate discreet ruthless perhaps at noon with naomi
but all between the four white walls of moderation
and not squeezed in against the backseat igloo roof of the toyola

just enough friends just enough spirit/s just enough cuff link/s
    showing
just enough legal cockspring from the king/size bed
no squalid secrets squeeling in the cup
board no niggers to his name no tingle tang or tri

angle no ting-ti-clang no jive clean
cleenex sheets clean slate his naaman coopper
plate in the guilt edge family buy/ble

the black puddin an house-spouse souse
far from temptations of eve
ning guardening up the vase of fat flowers
ring on that twinkeling fling/er

   do you remember lit/tle star
   how i wander where you are
   thy people shall be my people and thy gas my journey

and the pickney u/nique
natt/y natt/u nat/u/really and he
growing with the rhododendrons ob dem
the chickenlicken goodness ob dem

and listening for news of their delinquency
how they have dropped out gone
dreadlocks or rasta shacked
up with a shop

67

girl an callin her queen
sayin they playin guitar like marley or sparrow or
tosh an gettin arrest/ed for ganja or molotoff cock
tail or rub

a-dub sounn system dub wid a bomb tick
in soff in it belly like shaka guevara or kroff
or juss gorn porn pickin dumb

There is also the version of fathers
those who live on the dub side of mujeres

betroddin dem after the bram or durin the cyar-
nival season duck-

in dem into the dark room of sky juice an sweet talk an dry rub an
  kisco
after the unabandoned hard-on at the street corner disco

midmorning comes with streets of scuffle
runnin with the pack

for luck
pacin the competition

just sufferin farward with spike an heel an i:ron
trying to keep dat piss/tol hot an hard an heavy

the thrilldrens here are feathers in a hat-
trick or medals upon

idi amins chest
no more no less

noon brings the dread dark glasses rhygin hat
ites goatee beard jah voice and i-man gait
here is the fate/al of survival or salvation

ruler of rod and zion
juggler of lead and life/force
hustler of licks and rickets

he uses rape as ransome
as totem pole against the future of old age that he will never reach
so young so caul so ital and so handsome

his afternoon of sunsets bleeding in the gutter dries swiftly with
  the stain of voices of his victims children

The sons rose to their whiteness of noon and the scars fell. we would never be

prodigal mennen. the plantation ground would not be a play-ground for ever and we could never own that silver hush of cane those lorries growling up the hill those

shadowed walls among the casurines. school went so far and no father. book didnt ring bell with the school bill. to learn was a wave up the slope of the beach and slipping back down to dark water. so we had to find work: mechanic clerk police/man

tief. make a good start and hurt yuself up from the button. no time for the sun/light. darkness of words: talk at de corner talk talk talk in de rumshop talk after church of first sundees talk talk talk about talk about how we owns nothin. talk about nothin. nothin. mothers gave us their milk until we were married or marred:

often both: until we became the child of our women: sucking their love sulking spoilt little battoes in spats. the houses we lived in were rented. pay packet empty by freddies. food cigarette bettin shop races de wife in a turn an me monthly down pun a cycle. that at least i is own: a good tickin raleigh bicycle. nex she wantin a singer sewing machine: no hann fangle ting: she wantin a black one wid pedal. so

we walkin out good till de firss baby come: bonnet pram bootie wettin de bed: evry body stannin rounn cooin like woo-dove: look how e favour e faddah they sayin: look e lil booee eye an e twiss mout. an e big bubby muddah got e chattel up safe an fat in she out a harms way. so is family now an i owns it.

i owns it? more cow an gate food an a carry cot fuh de fella an nobody hey mindin i. an wha bout a house a we own: shed roof an a little latch on: is to get piece a lann an who own it. doan mine it is rab: yu watchin dat grass piece brawlin back there: wid de stick-yuh-toe weeds an de little mauve flowers among it: yu thinkin i owns it? dat paff dat dere now: runnin way from yu goin up de hill rounn de benn by miss brevitor tree: yu tinkin i owns it? we u:sed to run up there fass fass fass   we bare feet spinnin like bicycle wheels   de singin angel kite in me hann already ablaze wid de rainbow a heaven. who block off de paff an rip up de kite when it pitch down? where de pond water gone wid de frogs an de mornin stars? who fence in de gully wid cat wire? who put up dat sign sayin

KEEP OUT

and de green white purple an blue a de sea stain wid oil. dis kinda question is pedal me mine. it is ride i

KEEP OUT

uh pushin back home thru de rain wid me brain soakin wet. who gwine dry me?

KEEP OUT

since she gone out dese days to ketch work: so she sayin: tryin to mek enns meet: she is leff de meat in de turn-down heat oven warmin up cole. de way i feel she cud fry me. a

dry stick stickin up lonely. even de boy almost bigger dan i is aready. he bigger dan i is aready. de grass growin green de trees growlin bloomer de sky full a breeze an it

bluer. is only i gettin smaller. somethin squeezin i head like a sorringe. uh drink it an dry. is de sun dyein out of i vision. no man i never did own it. cause a man cyan be

faddah to faddah if e nevvah get chance to be son/light

IX

RETURN OF THE SUN

29

i
Pssssssss
said the leaves

and adam looked up
and saw her there on the branch of the tree

want thum duncks? she
began/throw

ing him one which he caught without looking/he
was watching her there on the branch of the tree/her

face and her neck and her bodice
were sprangled with shadow and light from the tree/*what*

chu watchin me for she
pretended pretending the wind made her hold her skirt

down   every move
ment she made   was call

ing upon his attention/*why*
yu dinn come lass night? she

didn't reply so he asked her a/
gain *why yu dinn come lass night/yu*

wath there/how yu mean i was there! wha
else yu expec a/

73

dam told her/ she
threw him more duncks one after one after one after one very
   quick/

ly so that he had to catch them all quick/
ly *i*

thaw yu she
said it very off handed busily stretching through shallows of glass

he could feel the morning hot on his face as he watched
her/cooled by the scramble of crabs cross his forehead

and his heart was beating like sun/light like sun/light

yu saw me yu saw me yu saw me yu say an/
she bit softly into the dunck she was smile

ing and laughed him. she
had a hard way of laugh/ing with a little lilt at the end

an i waited an waited she
made him feel like a fool and she knew

it

yu wath waithin fuh some/thin?
she mocked him *stannin*

up they by de corn/
er c'dear/why yu cunnn keep yuself quiet nuh man

yu inn know evahbody cud theee it was yu/but i
dinnn see yu: whey

yu was!/whey i wath? whey i wath? re
peating his questions was one of the ways she would tease

him and her eyes disappeared into bright little twinkles of
   sun/light

74

so he asked her again *why*
yu dinn come lass night/be

cauth she
began and dangled her silence down from the tree

cause why a/
dam pressed

her: a game where they tied
up yu eyes an yu had to guess

who yu ketch/

in *be*
cauth why before zed she

was laugh/ing she say
yu

want my mutha to beat
me/yu

*what/*a
dam said *my*

mutha she
said *yu*

inn deaf yu
inn dead yu

want she to beat
me she said

an is all de fault a yu uncle/my
uncle! but what is dis now *wha*

wrong wid my uncle! he was very pride
a e uncle

e does drive the lorry too reck
leth she told him *yu*

inn hear bout wha happnn
how de lorry mek duss like a shirt tail flappin

an we swingin de corners fass fass fass
an de trees dat we pass goin *mash up an red*

man foot get cruth in de bar
ginn all de way down to six mens bay

so muh mutha say is a cathe in court
an we isunth to thpeak nor have nuthin to do wid

ooona she
said showering down more duncks from the tree

but i see yu dis mornin in granfadda shop! swallow
ing hope like he drowning he drowning *i know*

esse say

but ith only becauth we cunnn get no corn
meal to buy from any place elth in this hickey

she say

an yu know how corn/meal scarcer than chrithans these days esse
say

trying to sound like her mother

but she warn me an warn me she warn me an thay that i wuthant
    to how

thedoo nor goodmorninmam to no niggerman in yu granfatha
    shop esse

said pricking her hand on a plimpler and sucked
it

76

ii

and adam remembered the morning when the sun was still a cool
humpty dumpty over the akee tree and the tamarind tree which
bore a seed with the face of the man who had died where the tree
was now (so the beachboys said) and had seen far away where the
sky was low a big bright wave that was standing still *anamabu
cape coast kromantin castle* but was building up and was getting
bigger and he tried to run but the water pulled him back when he
tried to run and his sister screamed and his mother held her close
as she turned her back to the cruel sea and the world was falling
like the power of babel and a mortar was pounding *makola
makola makola makola* as he opened his eyes to his mother
sprawled but still hugging his sister in the pool her arms made and
her yellow bathcap bobbin

    for mothers stood in the light of the door
    way mothers stood at the end of the yard

    mothers were *loa* were stone crabs were fish traps of no
    they were pebbles of sound down the floor of a well

    you couldn't fight mojers you couldn't shout mojers
    you couldn't even smile mojers down

and esse's mudda was tall tin an raky cutting flame all day in de
  canefields

an carry it carry it carry it carry it swingin home hard like a bell in
  her heart

i
*But yu still want to drive
it?/* he

started not able to follow this sudden tack
in her mean

ing *my
lorry* she lisp

ered sitting down on the branch of the tree

he could see the promised land of her thighs as she sat with her
    skirt like a cat
up her legs and the skin of her shiney and smooth and smelling of
    duncks

tree/*yu
lorry?* he

still couldn't follow the swing of her feet in the sweet of the tree
    like

yu this/
ter she told

him and before that bubble was bold in his head

*uh lookin some/body to drive
it/yu*

know a good drive/
er glitt

ering down from the bram
bles/the leaves of her bodice

sparkle from spangle to shadow to dark
in the hool of that muse/ical tree

an who gwine pay fuh de gas a/
dam asked her still try

ing to follow but fall
ing/*de gath*!

she cried *haee* clapping her hands together like shakshak

o this had her now she was happ/y o jeeesus shine she was happ/y
he was talking her own langridge now and he had her he had her
he had her/he thought she would fall from the heave/of the tree

*an inn yu gwine screw/off de cap a de bonnick yu thay yu is man
and crank up de fan wid dat handle yu handl/e an pump/it* she
laughed him and then like wind with a cloud brings a sudden
change to the canefields breathing grey where there once had been
green esse say

*yu theee/yu theee/yu theee what uh thell yuh! dah is all yu ramgoats
wantin wid we/pump yu gaths up de tank an is not even tanks
like muh mutha say an aftha yu finish drive bout like yu like/oona
gone back to town when yu dun an fuhget bout de bill when a
accident come an de lorry dey pun de dump/heap   but lithen to
me mith/ter john belly guts no/body int drive thith lill lorry yet*
showing him where it was in the tree *an no/body inn gettin no
chance to-rit neida unleth they kin show me thuh lithunse*

her lips curved and curled drinking the shade and the shadow and
she spat out a dunck seed *thoo* through the air and hit him hard
on the forehead

then she said the cloud drifting off its breeze dragging light like a
boy with e lorry

yu know de lath letter yu senn me i loothe it she say her voice like
the soft underdrone of the leaves her face fading further and
further in shadow and she had him goin rounn like a clock going
back/wards *it loth* esse

say *an suppose somebody to fine/it* he told

her *suppothes suppothes always suppothes yu inn know that all pothes and nuh topthies doan work*

her face coming back from its

shadow *it was they all the time/had um fole up near the faith a me hymn book where i ith keep the sundee school pic/tures*

musse drop outa they when uh walk back dung de hill from the church/yard she

say *an yu didnt look for it?* big-able now and he liked
it

uh walk evry step back an fort back an fort from muh house to de church/yard tree times esse said

from her house to the churchyard was more than a mile and he knew

it

*uh look evry where/an inn fine
it?/*she

didnt reply swimming away to the high

of the tree *uh sorry*
he said trying to dive up the sky

of her tree

*but uh doan tink no body gwine fine
it* he

said *then
uh glad* esse

say *no
body gine fine*

it?/yu
sorry she

said jumping down from the sky
of the tree

yu int know he
began stopped and start/ed

again *yu*
int know a/

dam said
yu isnt to jump-dung like dat from a tree

weeeeeeeeee she reply her eyes open wise
ly *yu frighten i break*

it? reach
ing tip toe for the basket of duncks in the y of the three

an i isnt to see yu to see yu to see yu she turned the summertime

tang in her arms and she close to him isnt to close to him close to
him close to him now he could see her eyes now her small dark-

brown and quick/ly not hidden away from him now she was close
to him close to him close to him now like flowers of sadness of

shadows of silence like on the floor of a pool

but suppose yu mother to ketch yu he
teased her but frighten

an suppoth your nothe wath a dirthy ole pothe
and she pushed

him but he caught her hand by the hand that had pushed
him and held

81

her

leh
me
go
leh
me
go
leh

me

GO

and she gave a sweet tug as she cuffed the word

GO

but he held/as her teeth bit into his finger and

aaee a/
dam cried but he held

her and
yu

she was breath/less

yu
yu
yu

she was almost now help/less her face burn/ing hot like the sun
light her plaits wild and rest/less her breath/less a fish flappin bout
at the end of a line in he hann *i gwine*

BUTT

yu she shout/ed he took the blow hot full from her forehead into the muscle just over his bell/y the rain of the duncks tree fall/ing and fall/ing he

held her one hand like a hand/cuff hard round her wrist the other one round the sweat pride of her neck as he held

her

yu

esse said

yu
yu
yu

esse said

soft
er
and

soft
er
and
soft
as he kissed

her

yu face hot he managed to murmur trying to catch the moth of her cheek that was flutt/ering under the pain of his fingers she close to him close/r the cane/fields spinning slowly around him the whole shape of the world stretching lazily out in the heat and the sweet of the duncks of her skin curving down sweeter and sweet as she pulled herself free closer and closer and picked up her basket and left

him

ii
       and

amen was all she could say
       when the lawyers told her there wasnt a will
       that her husband had died in his testicles

amen was all she would say
       when they came with their vans to take way the four poster
         bed
       with the big brass knobs where she had been born
       where she herself had been bred

       that should have been as she said her final faithful consoler
       the walnut sideboard where the wares were and the wine
         glasses still
       wrapped up in straw that had been her wedding pediments

amen amen was all she could say
       when they took the mahogany table away
       polished until it was almost as black as her face
       in it looking up at her face in it year after year after year

amen for all the vows that she grave
       for the pleasures that she gave/away
       for the promises he played upon her gramophone

amen to the plans for the extra shed-roof she had paid for
       for the wax in e ears when e ears wouldnt lissen to she
       for that wax/inkernel of pain in e belly that hardened his
         eyes to a glisten

       she sang the hymn without tune without words with long
         hot pregnant pauses
       chugging the milk into butter
       hugging its warm animal mutter closer and closer and
         closer

       and

amen was all she could say
        to the back and the break and the breeders of strife

amen to the wind and the fish and the cool of the knife
amen *amen* to their love and the men in her life

        promises
        promises
        promises

X

FLECHES

31

i

Still i suppose he married well: the wedding picture shows a quiet con-
fidence: tight grip on the icing cake bri-
dle bold look into the few-

ture: the close shaved well brushed head
the dark famed glasses. there were,
unless i'm wrong, no other family pic-

tures: except the one with me i found already faded
framed among the cuff links and the round hard collar leather
    boxes
in his dresser in the bedroom with the simmons bed with springs

i made a trampoline. this pic-
ture shows him always suited dressed for work hat
on his head no light between his him and me

looking out into the cameras of glass with the same quiet
wedding pic-
ture confidence and me just three

my mother say is almost tall as he al-
ready standing up pun a canebottom chair
in what they call a bib for drib-

ble: sticky wet protein that reach my belly
button; nip-
ple shape mouth sticking to my thumb

and naked doggie pee/ping out between my bandy legs
for all the world to see.
this photograph was taken at a man-

sion house my mother said she'd borned me in:

a place i didn't know a time i can't remember
how could they take a memory of time i can't remember
how could i have been there and yet forget

so that i used to sit and stare at us for hours going through the
    dresser drawers
that pulled out softly sweetly cedar mothballs camphor
given him the day he married by his uncle ogoun carpenter
my treasure chest assyrian illicit east

my labyrinth to truth perhaps pursuit of past and future
    knowledge
and there were letters there old papers folded over
some tied and all dried up i
could not/would not read them

cufflinks of pearl it seemed
and onyx cold tie pins
even more colden tie clips
as delicate and pristine as the newest moon grown gold above the
    setting browns beach sun

and nuggets that he throttled to the throat of his hard collar
    collars

and at last a little pill box where he kept his silver six-
pences: milled edges oaktreeleaf britannia
as beautiful and light as wafers that the priest put on miss sissies
    tongue
on certain saddened sundays

if he knew that i took them one by one first
just to borrow then to keep help
me to buy brown bus stand nuts and sugar-
cakes and cockies: he never said he knew and never
said he missed them: perhaps he never missed

them: the dresser drawers were sweet and smooth al-
ways unlocked but i had never seen him open them
or wear a tie or shirt or pearl white cuff
link from in there or even check his papers: why

though one day hiding seven six-
pences beneath a stone in our back-
yard: my static fence my transit station to the world
of crime: the silver prints just disappeared and my guilt
grew like crab grass trails along the borders of our yard

what else remains is fragments: his leather belt reluctantly pulled
    out
like a steam engine from its track around his waist
when he came home from work on orders from my mother
who'd tried in vain to catch me: he

mus wash de boy in licks now now: his
bringing home: was it at christmastime: the village
choirs swimming down the road with lanterns: *ajax*
achilles: singing their white hushed ships upon the land like xy
    lophones

canadian english apples red-
der than the holly on our x-
mas cards: and was there jelly

on them: and purple grapes
cold with the ice house vapour
on them with their own light

within them and nitt-
y spit out bones from lebanon from algeceiras
from sunny countries sunnier than hours

and green hills far away

ii
it was a time and tide that brought us close
to christ to chrystal glass to no-
man's heaven and of course i-scream

though he bought bajan too
at least my mother esse would complain
uh cyan begruge de fac e was a good pro-
vider lawd be praise

brown purity bakery bread still breathing from the oven and ihs
    holy name*amen*
in great brown paper bags we tried to run
sack races in and fruit as precious as those six-

pences: star apple sugar
apple akee pawpaw pa-oui lakatan
fat pork and soursop and sapodilla eyes

and sometimes wrapped up in a ole fishscale news-
paper: a whole smooth dolphin's archery of flight through
    underwater rainbows' colours drying out
or a redtail cavallee

fish

was a sign of peace inside our house
we listened in the dark to how our mother quarrelled all night
    long like surf
lines on the other shore: he never angered we could hear

though sometimes coughed and sometimes terrible to fear: what
would become of us: said
he would go back out and *stay* back out: our mojer bawled

then silence

at last the crickets chirped the bull frogs bulbed
the night wind nestled in the black leaf tree

and i could hear that big land crab that dreamed beneath the
    rock-stone where i lay my six-
pences creak out and crackle over almond leaves: the next day

fish

XI

INDIGONE

32

i
Now we is all gathered here at grandfather's hoom in the small
  front room in the house
in the country where the rains
came down and the ponds were big with its photographs of
  daughters in white organdie:

hands touching gently the artificial vase
of flowers: in white socks: since everything was blackandwhite the
  memory
of cofflewalks and shackles my sister with her teddybear her eyes
  black liquid dew

drops and technicolour-tinted-behind-glass: joe louee with his
  powderpuff the dionne-
ese quin/triplicates with soap grandfather did not sell the royal
  family
in sundaypowderpink a rosicrucian EYE staring from rays of
  cloud that quite trans/
figured me and above the doorway into where we ate CHRIST IS
THE HEAD OF THIS HOUSE

a gramophone its corrugated trumpet silver handle spinning
  dog/such faithfulness it
heard it made you sick: *red sails in the sun/set/when the roll* and
  i'll be dead when
you glad you rascal you: okeh and *victor vox trot vox trot vox*
  trot blue bird and *his*
masters vice the radio that worked on uncle's lorry batteries and
  rocking chairs

of ethiopian lions that ogoun carved and cared for during the
    earth tremor of selassie's

war

the window in the little redwood gallery where i'd sit for hours
watching the canefields groan the blackbirds march across the
    road
the sun swing downwards to the shakshak
tree the mulecarts creak/ing home the way
the donkey dung was trod and round and burst like pods along
    the golden ground

and nighttime when the crickets became stars
and comets smoked high up among the betujels and jewels of
    orion and the flare of mars
the lighthouse distant beyond distance beyond fields
now silvery like nerves in darkness like quixote with his lance of
    light
searching for salt for dead souls for

we were dead: the us/not us: the dust: blood
spilled: green branches of the family bone cut off
from root and rib and culture: grand
father dead my father's further genitor
of futures past my borning ancestor

still burning in a room he'd left and still lay in:
a window open on his face so we could see and not
see him could recognize and not know him: be
coming *mmmmm*: the candle and the wax and ashes
and the closed cold ingrown ice face of that doll they'd placed in
    there

that could not look back out: six feet of him six feet deep down
    already in
the centre of that whirlpool room. we moved around his hool and
    silent howl
and rule and role of darkness: eyeless and leafless: graze/less

and we were there/not there the undertaker anxious with his mop
   and kerchief
screw/driver hammer ready for the wrench and damp and
   everlasting itch
but mek e bide a lil bit more aunt evvy said *he int goin down de*
   road dis time to soon come back

and i looked up to see my father's eye: wheeling towards his
   father
now as i his sun moved upward to his eye
brow lifted clear and high above his i

     trying to fend off the fear he was fearing
     the pain that was pealing his head like a bell
     the eyewater filling his skull like a shell

that ole rugged cross and that scarecrow

     fragments of error/fragments of bone
     but always that look confident now and un/broken
     shattering the rain/blow

ii
but suns don't know when they die
     they never give up
     hope heart or articule

gases gathered far back before they were born
     before their fathers dived down the shore of the dawn

       storing up their megalleons of light
       colliding with each other, hissing their white sperms of
         power
       and continue to steam, issue heat, long after their tropic
         is over

       so that they sweat, fevers of light years away
       though the age freezes over their eye
       though their intemperate i:ron has already wrinkled to
         rust

and the dead son, ex-
          plosionless socket
          collapses slowly into its shrinks

and the stars, soft watches of night
          fires of lizards and moths that loved power
          gravitational cool of your arm/pits

          weep tears of light
          for the memories, warmings of ecstasy, head tossed
          in the hollow of pillow they cried out was love

while others, more distant, further from that howl and hammer

seek newer longer more elliptical orbits
crabs cassiopeas andromedas
black lidded electronical caves bulg
ing with star-dust

but the boy walking the beach of his birth this day does not know
     this
          yet
and there is no one able to tell him this
          yet

stepping on bird toes blind eyes of wet feet winning towards his
     love

XII

SON

33

Water went
they say

land was not
they say

breath only then
they say

mountains were not
they say

stones neither
they say

nor fish
nor crab
nor shaegoe

the wind was al-
most but not yet

they say

like the rain
they say

there was no beach
nor the sound of breakers

there was no sound
they say

the dark had not gone
away

and out of this dark came nam
nameless dark horse of devouring morning

devouring the water that was not yet
they say

devouring the land that was not yet there
they say

until there was nothing there
until there was no nothing there
until there was meer

and so water came back
they say

and altered the dark
they say

with a whisper called salt
they say

with a tremor called whale
they say

with a slow rising light of leviathan
with a thunder called firmament

and the salt became stars
they say

and the light grew

and opened the eye of its flower
they say

out of that i-
sis

they say

out of that brass
that was beating its genesis genesis genesis genesis

out of the stammering world

and the dark went
they say

and the water coloured the land with ihs hum
they say

with ihs peril
they say

with ihs coral
they say

and my thrill-
dren are coming up coming up coming up coming up
and the sun

new

NOTES

I   RED RISING: dawn, the first voice of the rainbow.

Page 1

l.4. *hillaby soufriere and kilimanjaro*: mountain landmarks of the Third World: Hillaby, Barbados (though less than 1,000 ft!); Soufriere, St Vincent, active volcano; Kilimanjaro, Tanzania.

l.9. *sun/sum: sunsum*: Akan word for soul, origin of spiritual life.

l.11. *ihs*: natural/divine version of its/his

l.16. *mews*: sound-word (news/mews)

l.17. *origen*: origin, *originem*, and the Early Christian (Neo-platonist) theologian of Alexandria (c. 155–253). The 'rainbow' sense (literal, moral, mystical) of 'origin'.

Page 2

l.3. *iises*: Rastafarian version of 'praises'. *Jah, love* and *thanks* are also Rasta ritual words, juxtaposed here with N. American Indian sacred colours: black, blue, yellow, red.

Page 3

l.19. *hool*: hole, whirlpool, galactic black hole.

II   ORANGE ORIGEN: the second voice of the rainbow.

III SON: aspect of Sun.

Page 11

l.1. *browns beach*: main setting of poem — the sunset side of the island (in contrast with Atlantic sea coast of *Mother Poem*).

Page 15

l.1. *batto*: nickname (see note to p. 19, l.4 below).

l.11. *hickey*: Bajan (Barbadian) for wooded gulley wasteland behind villages; 'a place into which good manners and genteel customs have never penetrated' (Frank Collymore, *Barbadian Dialect*).

IV YELLOW MINNIM: *minnim*: 'caliban' for *minim*, the note value, associated with piano lessons, hence young, small, learning. *Yellow Minnim* suggests early morning (yellow light) and young, learning time. See p. 19, l.6 *mmofra* (children), *sprats and sprays* (small fish, minnow).

Page 19

l.3. *black bess*: Bajan place-name, and word for a 'strong woman'.
bussa: leader of the Bajan slave revolt of 1816 in parish of St Philip. (See poem 23, and note to p. 56. l.7 below.)
l.4. *bateau*: lozenge-shaped flat-bottomed boat (and see nickname, *batto*).
l.7. *tin*: thin, but with sense of tin (galvanized roofs and palings) also intended.
l.12. *kente*: W. African (Akan/Asante) woven cloth of colourful symbolic design. The Bajan patchwork apron worn by field-labour women and certain wayside sellers looks like *kente*.
l.17. *forgotten divinations*: the ritual use (pick up, click up) of sticks, seeds, pebbles is an aspect of African divination, still found in parts of the New World/Caribbean, but often now converted (forgotten) into a game: *warri*, pick-up-sticks, etc. *Warri/Owarre* is also a game in Ghana and parts of Nigeria, played with horse-nicker seeds. (See Collymore, op. cit., Cassidy/LePage *Dictionary of Jamaican English*, and R.S. Rattray, *Religion and Art in Ashanti*.)
l.18. *romie*: Bajan for card game, rummy.
suck-de-well-dry-dry: a simple card game.

Page 20

l.9. *barnabas collins*: the Dracula anti-hero of the N. American television soap horror, *Dark Shadows*.

Page 21

l.16. *petties* (or taws): crab claws.
l.17. *fromits*: thin frothy substance from crab mouth when angry or frightened.
1.19. *redge*: edge of ridge (see *hackletons cliff*, note for p. 52 below).
l.21. *old harbour* (Jamaica), *cartagena* (the Spanish Main), *tenoctitlan* (now Mexico City), *half moon fort* (Barbados): significant places in Caribbean/New World history.

99

Page 22

l.1. *mosquito one mosquito two*, etc: poem based on a folk, ring, or counting game.

l.8. *lix*: licks.

l.12. *de pine*: sugarcane estate near Bridgetown, legendary for *wild men in de canes*.

Page 37

l.23. *hoom*: an empty home, memory of home.

V THE CROSSING: the Middle Passage in reverse.

VI NOOM: the sound of noon; angelus of doom.

Page 48

l.5. *crink*: sound-word connected with eating; the sound of teeth against gristle and bone, or of gristle against bone, suggesting wrinkle of pain.

cavicle: A 'calibanism' for clavicle; the cave between neck and collar-bone.

Page 49

l.5. *tong*: tongue and instrument of torture.

l.15. *naygars*: dreadest niggers.

Page 51

l.8. *loa*: spirits, divine powers, gods. The word is from Haitian *vodun* and is probably of Fon origin.

l.11. *dreadren*: Rastafari brothers, known as 'dreads' or 'locksmen', who wear their hair natural (long, and matted).

l.13. *legba*: Fon/Haitian crippled god of the crossroads/*limbo*.

Page 52

l.15/16. *hackletons cliff*: prominent highland area overlooking Barbados' east coast (Bathsheba, Cattlewash); the site of *Mother Poem*.

Page 53

l.7. *pumpkin*: food staple, like yam, with religious attributes.

l.9. *love-vine*: a wild running parasite, often found on fences and along the borders of poverty.

l.17. *shango*: Yoruba and Black New World god of lightning and thunder.

l.18. *ogoun*: Yoruba and Black New World god of iron and invention, and complementary with and so inseparable from Shango in the 'destructive-creative principle' (see Wole Soyinka, *Myth, Literature and the African World*). One of their (technological) apotheoses is the train. The jazz rhythms of John Coltrane (see below) and the forward gospel impetus of Aretha Franklins (see below) are other aspects of this.

l.22. *aretha*: Aretha Franklin, queen of Soul.

l.25. *coltrane*: John Coltrane, master jazz saxophonist of the 'sixties; placed here with Aretha and Jesse Owens among the *loa*.

Page 55

1.2. *ifa's divination*: Ifa, Yoruba god/dess of wisdom and divination, had ihs oracle according to legend, at the centre of the world, in Ile-Ife, in what is now Nigeria (see also note to p. 19, l.17 above).

1.3. *maasai*: East African warrior and nomadic cattle people, famous, in the shadow of Kilimanjaro, for their height, grace, beauty, and for their diet of milk and blood.

Page 56

l.7. *bussa*: Bussa's slave revolt (1816), one of the very few reported for Barbados, started in the parish of St (Sin) Philip, where *Mother Poem* begins, at a place called Penny Hole (now Gemswick). Bussa, black, was aided by a free (?) mulatto called Washington Franklin, who until recently was given sole credit for the revolt.

Page 59

l.4. *shaego*: 'An attempted phonetic rendering of sherigo, a small sea crab which is found in shallow water near the beaches and which sometimes nips the toes of bathers.' (Collymore, op. cit.).

l.7. *ganja*: marijuana.

l.11/12. *a fair field...an no favour*: words attributed to Bussa.

VII   BLUE LOA: afternoon; decline of the *loa*.

VIII CLIPS: eclipse; film clips.

l.25. *pickney*: Caribbean version of Portuguese *pequenino*, N. American *pickaninny*, W. African *pickin*, all meaning 'small child', the Portuguese itself probably coming from W. Africa.

l.2. *mujeres*: mojers, mothers, women.
l.5/6. *sky juice* and *kisco*: sweet iced drinks.
l.18. *rhygin*: legendary Jamaican gunman (one of the first) celebrated in the film and novel, *The Harder They Come*.
l.19. *ites*: Rasta word of approval
l.26. *ital*: Rasta for 'pure', 'clean', 'vital'; food (root and vegetable) prepared without salt, used here like *ites* as a word of approval, meaning 'with a certain style'.

l.18. *freddies*: a Friday (fridee) eating place.
l.19. *a turn*: 'partner'; small self-help co-op organized mostly by women. Each month or pay-day a different partner collects the collective subscription.
l.25. *booee*: the pupil of the baby's eye.

1.22. *sorringe*: a sour (or sorry) orange.

IX   RETURN OF THE SUN: following the (e)clips(e), with the sense of prodigal as in the parable.

l.11. *ooona*: Igbo and Bajan/Caribbean for *you-all, all-yu*.

l.2. *pothes* (poes) and *topthies* (topsies): chamberpots, potties.

l.23. *wax/inkernel*: a growth (that does not wane?).

X FLECHES: flesh, flashes of sunlight, Amerindian rainbow feather crests.

Page 88

l.11. *uncle ogoun carpenter*: see note to p. 53, l.18 above. And also the poem 'Ogun' in *Islands*.
1.32/3. *sugar-cakes* and *cockies*: home-made sweets sold by wayside sellers.

Page 90

l.1. *bajan*: Barbadian.
l.10. *pa-oui*: variety of mango; *lakatan*: variety of banana.

XI INDIGONE: gone into indigo; the tone of indigo.

Page 91

l.1. *hoom*: see note to p. 37, l.22 above. Used here because of death.
1.9. *cofflewalks*: trails along which chained (coffled) Africans walked to the barracoons and jesus ships of the faulked atlantic crossage. See *clink coffle coffin* (p. 54, 1.26).
l.11. *joe louee*: Joe Louis, Afro-American heavyweight boxing champion of the 'thirties and 'forties.
l.12. *powderpuff*: as applied to Joe Louis: soft dynamite boxing gloves. But we are also in a general goods shop.
l.12/.13. *the dionnese quin/triplicates*: Canadian multiple births of the 'forties, their much celebrated faces found on advertisements for soap, etc.
l.19/20. *spinning dog*: His Master's Voice (recording company) logo.
l.21. *red sails in the sun/set; when the roll [is called yonder]*; i'll be *dead when you glad you rascal you* (Adam's inversion of Louis Armstrong's 'I'll be glad when you dead...'): record tunes on old 78s.
l.23/5. *okeh, victor, vox* (trot), *blue bird* and *his masters vice* (voice): gramophone record labels.

Page 92

l.2/3. *selassie's war*: the Emperor Haile Selassie's defence of Ethiopia against Mussolini in the 'thirties. 'Lion' (Selassie) is symbol of Ethiopia. The Rastafari movement is said to have started as a result of this war thanks to the publicity given to Selassie after it: 'a king shall come out of Africa'.

XII *SON*: Afro-Cuban folksong form.

Page 96

1.3. *nam*: soul, secret name, soul-source, connected with *nyam* (eat), yam (root food), *nyame* (name of god).

l.11. *meer*: smear (mere) of saltwater (*mare*), and sense of 'mother' too.